For Isolde and Oscar, my little monsters—K. E.

For my good friend, Freda—S. M.

2004 First U.S. edition

Myths and Monsters copyright © 2004 by Frances Lincoln Limited

Text copyright © 2004 by Katie Edwards

Illustrations copyright © 2004 by Simon Mendez

All rights reserved, including the right of reproduction in whole or in part in any form.

Charlesbridge and colophon are registered trademarks of Charlesbridge Publishing, Inc.

Published by Charlesbridge

85 Main Street, Watertown, MA 02472

(617) 926-0329 • www.charlesbridge.com

Myths and Monsters was edited, designed, and produced by

Frances Lincoln Limited, 4 Torriano Mews, Torriano Avenue, London NW5 2RZ

Library of Congress Cataloging-in-Publication Data

Edwards, Katie.

Myths and monsters: secrets revealed / Katie Edwards ; illustrated by Simon Mendez.

p. cm.

ISBN 1-57091-581-4 (reinforced for library use)

ISBN 1-57091-582-2 (softcover)

1. Animals, Mythical. I. Title.

GR820.E39 2004

398.24′54—dc22   2003020660

Printed in Singapore

(hc) 10 9 8 7 6 5 4 3 2 1

(sc) 10 9 8 7 6 5 4 3 2 1

Illustrations done in acrylic paints on Bockingford paper

Display type and text type set in Wunderlich Medium, Lithos, Lettres Eclates, and Copperplate

Color separations by Imagescan

Printed and bound by Star Standard in Singapore

Katie Edwards • Illustrated by Simon Mendez

MYTHS AND MONSTERS

Secrets Revealed

ini Charlesbridge

CONTENTS

INTRODUCTION

Myths are stories that usually have some basis in fact, but have been embellished to sound more frightening or fantastic.

Hundreds of years ago, many of the animals we are familiar with today, such as rhinoceroses, antelopes, and elephants, were unknown to Western Civilization. Only a few brave explorers ventured into unchartered parts of the world, often catching a glimpse of strange, new creatures on their travels—and when something looks strange, it can seem scary and threatening.

Early explorers also discovered mysterious remains and tried to explain what they were. Scientists did not yet know that whole groups of extraordinary animals had lived, died, and become extinct long before human beings evolved, leaving only their fossils behind. So when, for example, explorers found fossilized shark teeth, they believed them to be tongues that had fallen from the sky and turned to stone during an eclipse of the moon. Ammonites, extinct marine mollusks once known as snake stones, were thought to be coiled, headless snakes. And fossilized sea urchins at one time were highly prized as magical snake eggs.

So the explorers returned home with tales of the fabulous beasts they had found. And, like a game of telephone, as their stories were told over and over again by different people, details often got changed or exaggerated.

In the following pages you will read the stories of 10 legendary creatures and discover the reality behind the myths.

ROC

A YOUNG MAN
named Sinbad, hungry for adventure,
joined some sea-merchants setting sail across
the Indian Ocean. On his second voyage he
found himself stranded on a lush tropical island.

As he explored, he came across an enormous white
egg. It was so large that it took Sinbad 50 paces to walk
around it. Suddenly the sky went dark. As Sinbad looked up,
a gigantic white bird, a bit like an eagle or albatross, flew down
and landed beside the egg.

Sinbad had heard tales of this amazing bird, known as a roc,
from sailors, and he decided to strap himself on to one of its massive
legs and escape from the island. The next day the roc flew off, carrying
Sinbad with it. When at last it landed in a deep valley, Sinbad untied
himself and continued on his travels.

We now know that stories of the roc are probably based on a giant bird nicknamed the elephant bird by Marco Polo, an Italian explorer who traveled across Asia about 800 years ago. The elephant bird became extinct over 300 years ago, but its fossilized remains reveal that it was the biggest bird that ever lived. At almost 10 feet, it was so tall that if it were alive today, it would be able to peer into the top of a double-decker bus. It laid eggs as long as your arm.

Although the roc that Sinbad met could fly, the real elephant bird could not. It was confined to its home of Madagascar, a rich tropical island off the east coast of Africa.

LAKE MONSTER

DEEP, MURKY LAKES are just as popular as the open ocean
for inspiring tales of underwater monsters.

Nessie, perhaps the world's most famous lake monster, is believed to live in Loch Ness in
Scotland. The biggest lake in the United Kingdom, it is also very long, extremely deep, and
contains peat, which makes the water murky. Viking sagas were the first to mention an
elusive lake monster, but during the last 70 years there have been many reported sightings
of a humpbacked creature in Loch Ness. Photographs have been produced as evidence, but
they tend to be distant and out of focus.

A lake monster called Ogopogo is thought to exist in Lake Okanagan in Canada, and
Mokele-Mbembe is a dinosaur-like creature believed to lurk in the swamps of central Africa.

We now know that the most convincing photo of Nessie, known as the surgeon's picture, is a fake. Taken in 1934, it was created using a small model. Sonar tracking surveys over the last 30 years have failed to reveal any large creature living in the lake. A plesiosaur that has survived from the dinosaur age is the most popular explanation for the monster—and four vertebrae believed to be from a 34.5-foot-long plesiosaur were found on the banks of Loch Ness in 2003. But these long-necked reptiles lived in the sea, not in freshwater. And if they had survived the last 65 million years, there would have to be enough of them to form a breeding population.

However, a proven example of a living fossil is the coelacanth. This large, deep-sea fish was thought to have been extinct for nearly 70 million years until one was caught, alive and well, in 1938.

Pythons could account for the Mokele-Mbembe sightings in the African Congo. These snakes can reach 32 feet in length. They sometimes enter the water to catch fish but keep their heads above the water to breathe.

CYCLOPSES were a race of one-eyed, man-eating giants in Greek mythology. (*Cyclops* means "round eye.")

In his epic poem the *Odyssey*, Homer tells the tale of the Greek leader Odysseus, ruler of the island of Ithaca. Odysseus was curious to meet the Cyclopses, so he sailed to their island. He was hiding in a cave when a Cyclops named Polyphemus entered with his flock of rams. Seeing the invaders, Polyphemus sealed the cave entrance, seized a few sailors, devoured them alive, and settled down to sleep.

Trapped in the cave, Odysseus sharpened a stake and plunged it into Polyphemus's huge eye. The ogre bellowed with pain as his eye hissed and sizzled. The next morning, Odysseus and the remaining sailors escaped and sailed away from the island under a shower of rocks hurled from the cliffs by the blinded Cyclops.

CYCLOPS

We now know that the Greeks discovered large fossil bones and teeth in caves on Mediterranean islands, which probably fueled their belief in giants. The large central hole in some of the skulls was thought to be the single eye socket of a Cyclops.

The Cyclops myth was believed until just over 100 years ago, when a French scientist named Georges Cuvier compared the fossil bones of the "giants" with the bones of living animals. He realized that skulls with a large central hole belonged to elephants, and the hole indicated the position of the elephant's trunk.

CHIMERA is the name for an imaginary beast made from parts of different animals. According to ancient Greek legend, the Chimera was a fire-breathing, female monster with a lion's head, a goat's body, and a serpent's tail. When she attacked local people in the mountains of Lycia (now part of Turkey), the king offered a reward for killing her. A boy named Bellerophon took up the challenge and, riding the winged horse Pegasus, hunted down and killed the beast.

Other legendary chimeras include the griffin (half eagle, half lion), the Centaur (half human, half horse), and the Minotaur (half human, half bull).

CHIMERA

We now know that despite all the myths, chimeras have never existed. The first dried skin of a platypus, an Australian egg-laying mammal, was sent to Britain over 200 years ago. People thought it was some kind of chimera, suggesting it was created by attaching a duck's beak to the body of a mammal.

Recent scientific advances in genetic technology have allowed us to create modern-day chimeras in the laboratory, such as the geep, formed from a sheep and a goat, and the cama, which has a llama mother and a camel father.

MERMAID

MERMAIDS were first mentioned in ancient Greek mythology, and stories about them continued to be popular throughout the Middle Ages. The mermaid has a woman's head and a fish's scaly tail and is often shown sitting on rocks, singing sweet songs.

Some legends tell how sailors, mesmerized by mermaids' beautiful voices, tried to follow them to their underwater paradise, only to be lured to their death. Other tales describe kind mermaids warning sailors of sea storms to come, bringing up deep-sea treasure for them, or granting their wishes.

We now know that when sailors caught sight of mermaids, they were probably seeing dugongs, manatees, or seals. Like humans, these animals are mammals. They have adapted to life underwater but still need to come up to the surface to breathe.

Dugongs and manatees are huge, streamlined creatures with paddlelike flippers, no legs, and a flattened tail. Dugongs live around the coast of northern Australia, while manatees are found in Florida, the West Indies, West Africa, and the Amazon Basin. Dugongs and manatees swim slowly and gracefully through shallow tropical waters, grazing on sea grasses.

Seals live in colder waters, but they also bask on rocks. From a distance, their postures and cries can seem human. Fleeting glimpses of these shy creatures through mist, sea spray, or cloudy water are likely to have perpetuated the haunting myth of "the maidens of the sea."

THE HYDRA of ancient Greek legend lived in coastal swamps.

It had nine heads: the main head was immortal and the other eight regrew if they were cut off. The hero Hercules was commanded to kill the monster. He did this by cutting off the Hydra's eight mortal heads while his nephew, Iolaus, set fire to the necks. Hercules then cut off and buried the immortal head under a stone.

The kraken was a Norwegian horned sea monster whose streaming tentacles were lined with jagged suckers. Sailors were afraid to disturb a sleeping kraken, believing it would swallow their ship whole and ooze black liquid if they fought it.

Tales have also been told of a sea serpent with a horse's head and a flaming red mane. One was said to have been washed up on the shores of Orkney, off the north coast of Scotland, in 1808. It was reported to measure 56 feet in length—longer than two buses.

SEA SERPENT

We now know that sightings of real but rarely seen sea creatures can explain many mythical sea serpents.

The giant squid is similar in many ways to descriptions of the kraken and Hydra. It can grow up to 65 feet long and usually lives in cold, dark depths of 3,200 feet or more. Little is known about these reclusive giants, but their remains have been found in the stomachs of sperm whales. From the dinner-plate-sized scars seen on sperm whales' bodies, it is thought that the giant squid lashes out with its suckered tentacles in an effort to avoid being eaten.

The oarfish, or ribbonfish, is a flat fish that can grow up to 26 feet long. It has silver skin with a scarlet fin running along its back and might have been mistaken for a sea serpent.

UNICORN

LEGENDS OF THE UNICORN describe a pure white, noble, solitary creature with the powerful body of a horse and a long straight horn jutting out from its forehead like a spear. People once believed that the horn had magical healing properties, especially against poison.

To find the unicorn, hunters searched the depths of the darkest forests where it was thought to live. To catch it, they took an innocent young woman into the woods. As soon as the unicorn saw the woman, it would run to her, lie at her feet, and rest its head on her lap. The woman would stroke the unicorn until it fell asleep. The hunters, who were hiding in the trees, could then capture the animal.

We now know that the idea of the unicorn may have been based on several other horned animals.

The Arabian oryx is an antelope with two slender horns, which could easily have been mistaken for a single one when the animal is seen from the side.

People once thought that the single horn of the Asian rhinoceros had miraculous healing powers. These fierce animals were often trapped using a trained female monkey: the monkey would scratch the rhinoceros's back and rub its belly until it lay down and hunters caught it.

The extinct giant rhinoceros also had an enormous horn in the middle of its forehead. Fossils of its skull and teeth have been found in Siberia. They look rather like a horse's skull, so they may have inspired unicorn tales.

STORIES OF BLOODTHIRSTY,

fire-breathing dragons have been told in parts of Europe for over 1,000 years.

The tale of St. George and the dragon is set in Libya. An evil, winged monster lurked there in a swamp, choking the countryside with its vile-smelling, poisonous breath. The king decided that the only way to stop his people from being terrorized was to sacrifice his daughter to the dragon. As she waited in terror, tied to a stake, a knight in silver armor galloped up on his horse and promised to save her. When the roaring, thrashing monster emerged from its lair, the brave knight killed it with his sword.

In ancient China, dragons were believed to be powerful, wise, and magical creatures that lived in the sky. Their fiery breath formed the clouds and their footprints made rain fall.

DRAGON

We now know that tales of dragons in China date back 2,000 years, to a time when large fossil bones were discovered there. These bones and teeth were often ground up and used as medicines. In 1842 the remains were correctly identified as dinosaurs, a word that means "terrible lizards." So-called dragon's teeth are still sold in China today, but they are usually the fossilized remains of extinct mammals such as the saber-toothed tiger and the three-toed horse.

More recent accounts of dragons come from travelers' encounters with giant living reptiles such as the man-eating Komodo dragon, with its thick scaly hide, flickering tongue, and poisonous bite. Found only on the islands of Komodo and Rinca in Indonesia, it is the world's largest living lizard and feeds on goats supplied by local people and visitors.

PHOENIX

THE PHOENIX was a magnificent mythical bird with a scarlet body, blue eyes, purple feet, and iridescent wings. It lived in the woods of Paradise and was said to need only air to survive.

Every 500 years, when it was time to die, the phoenix would fly to Phoenicia, in Syria, where it made a nest from twigs, cinnamon, and myrrh in the tallest palm tree. The next day, when the sun rose, its sparks would set the nest on fire. The phoenix would open its wings and begin a graceful dance of death in the flames. As it burned up, a new phoenix would appear from the ashes. The new bird flew to Egypt, carrying a ball of myrrh, then returned to Paradise for another 500 years.

We now know that the purple heron is the closest living bird to the phoenix. It has purple coloring, a crest on its head, and builds its nest at the top of tall trees. In ancient Egypt, where the legend of the sacred phoenix began, the purple heron was worshiped as a sun bird.

Tropical birds found in Asia—such as the golden pheasant and the bird of paradise—have colorful feathers similar to descriptions of the phoenix. Early travelers and traders may have taken these birds' skins back to Egypt. Myrrh, a sweet-smelling gum resin from trees in Africa and Asia, may have been used to preserve the skins, contributing to the myth.

YETI

FOR AS LONG as there have been dense forests and mountain ranges, stories have been told of wild, hairy giants lurking in them. The myth is so strong that the tree-swinging ape found in the forests of Borneo and Sumatra is called an orangutan, which means "wild man of the woods."

One of the most enduring "wild man" myths is that of the yeti, or abominable snowman, believed to roam the snowy slopes of the Himalayan Mountains. Local people say that yetis carry a magic stone in their left armpit, which the creatures throw at large animal prey to stun and kill them.

From the 1920s onwards, reported sightings of the abominable snowman increased as more and more mountaineers attempted to climb Mount Everest. One account claimed that a yeti stole chocolate bars from a tent. In the 1950s and 1960s a photograph of a yeti footprint and samples supposedly from the scalp and skin of a yeti were brought back to Britain for investigation.

We now know that the yeti footprint was probably made by a langur monkey, which often stands on two legs. Although this monkey leaves small footprints in fresh snow, if these impressions melt and refreeze several times, they can become enlarged and distorted.

When the yeti scalp and skin samples were taken to the Natural History Museum in London for identification, scientists discovered that the scalp came from a Himalayan serow goat and the skin from a blue bear. Blue bears are actually brown and live in Tibet.

It has been suggested that the yeti could be a distant relative of a giant ape called *Gigantopithecus*. These apes, which stood ten feet tall, lived in Asia until about 300,000 years ago.

GLOSSARY

ammonites [AM mah nites] Extinct marine mollusks with spiral shells.

Bellerophon [beh LER ah fawn] A Greek hero who killed the Chimera.

Chimera [ky MEER ah] (capitalized) A fire-breathing monster in Greek mythology with a lion's head, a goat's body, and a serpent's tail.

chimera [ky MEER ah] (lowercase) An imaginary beast made from parts of different animals.

coelacanth [SEE luh kanth] A fish dating back to the Paleozoic and Mesozoic eras.

Cyclops [SIGH klops] A race of one-eyed giants thought to have been shaped from fire and rock.

dragon [DRAG un] A mythical fire-breathing creature usually depicted with scales and wings.

dugongs [DOO gongs] Marine mammals that are also known as sea cows.

Hercules [HER cue lees] A Greek hero famous for his immense strength. Killing the Hydra was one of the twelve labors that Hercules was ordered to perform as punishment for killing his wife and children in an insane rage.

Hydra [HIGH drah] A monster from Greek mythology that had nine heads, one of which was immortal.

Iolaus [EE oh lay us] Hercules' nephew. He helped Hercules defeat the Hydra.

kraken [KRAH kin] A Norwegian sea monster.

lake monster [LAKE MON stir] A huge creature that lurks in a body of water.

Loch Ness [LOCK NESS] *Loch* is Scottish for "lake." Loch Ness is the United Kingdom's largest lake and is where the Loch Ness monster supposedly lives.

manatees [MAN nuh tees] Marine mammals with flippers and a rounded tail.

mermaid [MER made] Fantastic creature with the head and upper body of a woman and the tail of a fish.

Minotaur [MIH nah tahr] According to Greek legend, the Minotaur was the offspring of King Minos of Crete. Half bull and half man, the Minotaur was confined to a labyrinth, and every year 14 victims were sacrificed to him until the hero Theseus killed him.

Mokele-Mbembe [MOHK lay mm BEM beh] A lake monster that was said to live in the swamps of central Africa.

monster [MON stir] A strange and terrifying animal.

28

myths [MITHS] Traditional stories created to explain fantastic events, people, creatures, and ideas.

Odysseus [oh DIH see us] King of Ithaca and Greek leader who fought in the Trojan War. His adventures are told in Homer's epic poem the *Odyssey*.

Ogopogo [oh go POE go] A Canadian lake monster that supposedly lived in Lake Okanagan in British Columbia.

oryx [OR iks] African and Arabian antelope.

Pegasus [PEH ga sus] A winged horse in Greek mythology.

phoenix [FEE niks] A mythical bird that after 500 years was said to fly to Phoenicia and build a nest out of myrrh. The nest would become enflamed by the rays of the rising sun, killing the bird, which would then be reborn out of its ashes.

platypus [PLAT ih puhs] An aquatic mammal with fur, webbed feet, and a ducklike bill. The female platypus lays eggs.

plesiosaur [PLEE see uh soar] A marine reptile of the Mesozoic era.

Polyphemus [paw lee FEE mus] The son of the sea god, Poseidon, Polyphemus was a cyclops who was blinded by the Greek hero Odysseus.

roc [ROCK] An enormous bird that supposedly lived on a lush tropical island in the Indian Ocean.

Sinbad [SIN bad] A traveler from Baghdad who is featured in *The Arabian Nights' Entertainments; or, The Book of a Thousand Nights and a Night*.

St. George [SAINT JORJ] A legendary dragon slayer who is the patron saint of England, Lebanon, Canada, Palestine, Venice, and many other places. He is celebrated each year on April 23.

unicorn [YEW nuh corn] A mythical beast with the body of a horse and a long straight horn jutting from its forehead.

yeti [YEH tee] A hairy beast with human and apelike features believed to live in the Himalayas.